Marketing Plan
Template & Example

Alex Genadinik

DEDICATION

Dedicated to my mother and grandmother who are the biggest entrepreneurs I know.

TABLE OF CONTENTS

FOREWORD

Prior to starting any business, it is prudent to have a business plan and a marketing plan. Most first-time entrepreneurs find the overall process of starting a business so daunting that creating a marketing plan takes a lower priority. Without a marketing plan, the overall business strategy is incomplete, and this can cascade into a host of compounding problems. By getting this book, you are already ahead of the game because, by the end of this book, you will have a strong marketing plan and a stronger overall marketing strategy.

The advice in this book is based on my experience and success marketing my own business and the 1,000+ different businesses of my clients whom I either coached or helped promote directly.

Every great marketing campaign starts with a great marketing plan. In sharing the tips in this book, my hope is that you too will find marketing success and grow your business or anything else you hope to promote. I wish you the best of luck and hope that the ideas in this book will contribute to your success. Enjoy the book.

CHAPTER 1: INTRODUCTION TO MARKETING PLANS

"If you fail to plan, you plan to fail."

- Benjamin Franklin

1. Introduction to the book and how the book is structured

I appreciate that you got this book and I want to extend a very warm welcome to you. By the end of this book, you will be able to create a fantastic marketing plan. I hope you are excited about that since marketing is the key to growing your business.

This book takes an innovative and holistic approach to teach you how to create a marketing plan. To help you plan effective marketing campaigns, this book is split into five distinct parts.

Part 1: An innovative way to break the planning of different businesses into a few buckets and put correct marketing "modules" into those buckets. If you are a first-time entrepreneur or a first-time marketer, you will see how simple and eye-opening it will make your planning.

Part 2: You will start by making a 3-sentence marketing plan which will be the simplest way to get started.

Part 3: You will extrapolate your 3-sentence marketing plan to expand it into a 1-page marketing plan.

Part 4: We will look at my practical approach to the marketing plan of my own business.

Part 5: We will go over a real example of a full marketing plan, and I'll walk you through what to write in each section of the plan so that you can use it as a template to expand your 1-page marketing plan and turn it into a full and professional marketing plan.

This book will walk you through a ladder-like system where you start with just the 3-sentence marketing plan, grow that into a 1-page marketing plan and turn that into a full plan.

Most people have low confidence when it comes to creating their marketing plan. They usually struggle during the writing process. The struggle and low confidence typically lead to procrastination or outright quitting. The method in this book is meant to walk you through the planning process by starting with the very basic and building up your skills and confidence as you go.

In an effort to give you even more value, I added 3 additional free resources at the end of the book. Browse all the resources there, and take advantage of the free gifts.

With these extra freebies, the book has a balance of theory, practical examples, templates, and guides to aid you in writing your marketing plan.

Disclaimer: I use my own company's marketing plan in some examples in this book. I am not doing that to promote my business. The reason I use my company in the examples is that I know my company well, and I am able to give insightful examples with it.

2. What is a marketing plan

The *theoretical* definition of a marketing plan is a comprehensive document that outlines an organization's marketing (free promotion) and advertising (paid promotion) strategy for a given time into the future.

In *practical* terms, a marketing plan can be two things. The first and simple way to look at a marketing plan is as a strategy that you have in your mind without having anything written. The second way to look at a marketing plan is as a professional document that contains the strategies of how you will promote your business.

3. When and why you need a marketing plan

You don't always need a formal marketing plan document, but you must always have a very good and ultimately effective plan for promotion.

During your business planning phase, before you start doing actual work on your business, one of the biggest components of planning your business is creating a strong marketing plan that your business will implement.

Some types of businesses have few effective marketing strategies and some businesses have many. You must understand which marketing strategies will be effective for your type of business and your unique situation, and have a sense of how well those marketing strategies will do.

If you are working for an established business, your marketing department should have a full and professional marketing plan document with deadlines, budgets, and many additional details. Having that helps to make sure that everyone in your marketing department is on the same page, and for higher bosses to sign off on, and approve.

For new businesses, having a strong marketing plan (a document or mental plan) with effective strategies is extremely important because marketing is the lifeline of your business. If the strategies in the marketing plan will work, your business will grow. If your planned strategies aren't effective, your business won't grow.

See how your marketing plan can be a matter of life and death for your company?

4. First-time entrepreneur and beginner marketer mistakes

Most first-time entrepreneurs don't put too much thought into their marketing during business planning. They get excited about their business idea, plow into their business full speed ahead, and figure that they will sort out the details later as things come up.

If asked about how they plan to promote their business, most first-time entrepreneurs and first-time marketers say something that very closely resembles this:

"I will promote my business with business cards, fliers, and social media sites like Facebook and Twitter."

Does this sound a little bit like your plan to promote your business? This isn't really a plan. This is more of a sign that there is no actual plan. A real strategy is usually more nuanced and tailored to a unique business situation than simply choosing a few of the most apparent marketing ideas.

Don't worry. This is why you got this book. As you move through this book, you will refine your marketing plan to make sure that it isn't generic, but suited to your unique business, and will ultimately be effective.

The reason most first-time entrepreneurs repeat the one line "plan" above is simply that they don't know better. The more you will learn about marketing and the more comfortable you will become with it, the more refined your marketing plans will naturally become.

5. What makes a good marketing plan

In my opinion, what makes a good marketing plan isn't the formatting or the length of the document, but whether the chosen strategies are ones that will be effective in promoting and growing your business. After all, this isn't a school assignment. This is the real world and a lot is at stake.

If the marketing strategies are well-chosen, vetted, and created by savvy and experienced marketers, they have a greater chance of succeeding than strategies made by first-time marketers. That's why this book will "hold your hand" and guide you through the planning process step by step. By the end of this book you should be able to choose effective marketing strategies and create a solid overall marketing plan.

To help you with your marketing journey there are a few free gifts that can be found at the end of the book. My goal with these extra free gifts was to give you extra value in addition to the book itself. As one of the free gifts, I am happy to give you feedback on your marketing plan. When you create your 3-sentence marketing plan, that is the ideal thing to send me to look over. I'll help to make sure that you are on the right track.

CHAPTER 2: SIMPLE MARKETING PLANS FOR ANY BUSINESS

There are two marketing plan inventions in this book that will ease your planning. I've already touched on the 3-sentence marketing plan which is the first innovative aspect of this book. I'll help you create yours in this chapter.

The second innovative aspect of this book that I'll introduce you to is the "marketing buckets" concept which will help you choose the best marketing strategies for your business.

Here is how to ideally work through this section:

1) In section 1, create, write down and save your 3-sentence marketing plan

2) Go through the next sections of this chapter and see how to match the right "marketing buckets" to the kind of business you have

3) At the end of this chapter, create a new 3-sentence marketing plan, and compare it to your original plan to see the difference between them.

This 3-sentence marketing plan will contain the core elements of your overall marketing plan, and following this process will ensure that the core of your plan is correct and you are on the right track.

1. Let's start with the 3-sentence marketing plan

Many people ask for a big marketing plan template to fill out. The problem is that a big template is confusing, and most people get lost or stuck in the process and quit. Even if you do fill it out completely, it only helps you with the form and not the quality of your strategies.

To remedy that, I invented the three-sentence marketing plan. It works just like my 3-sentence business plan in case you've read the sister book to this one, which is my business plan book. The 3-sentence approach is great for first-time entrepreneurs. It helps you focus on the core aspects of your plan, and expand your plan almost like you would climb stairs: one step at a time rather than trying to take one big jump from the first floor to the top of the building.

Here is what each sentence in the 3-sentence marketing plan should be:

1) Tell what your business is

2) List of carefully chosen marketing strategies that will work to promote your business

3) How your product is different from competitors, your niche or your UVP (Unique Value Proposition)

Let's go through a couple of examples to make the writing of your 3-sentence plan clear. After that, you will create your own.

Example 1 (fictitious business):

Sentence 1: My business is a roofing business.

Sentence 2: I will promote this as a local service using local Google search, local listing websites such as Yelp, and by building a professional referral network with other home repair businesses.

Sentence 3: My business is different from other roofing businesses in the city because it serves affluent single-family homes with mostly solar panel installation.

The second example is the real marketing plan for my mobile app business. My apps have close to 2,000,000 combined downloads at the time of this writing. I never created a full-length written marketing plan. This 3-sentence marketing plan is essentially my entire mental marketing plan. The beauty of such simple planning is that if you focus on the right things to plan and identify correct promotion strategies, it works wonders and there is no reason to overcomplicate things by over planning.

Example 2:

Sentence 1: My business is a mobile app that helps people with business planning.

Sentence 2: I will promote through app store search, publicity, and social sharing.

Sentence 3: I'll differentiate from the competition by creating the most helpful business planning app that offers live expert help right on the app.

See how in just a few sentences you can lay out the foundation for your plan? The most important part is to correctly choose your set of marketing strategies and to choose differentiation wisely.

The main challenge for new business owners and first-time marketers is to know which strategies might work. If you are new to marketing, all the potential strategies to promote look pretty good. The challenge is to know which ones will actually work. This is where there is no substitute for having an experienced marketer on your team.

After you complete this chapter, you are welcome to email me and send me your three-sentence marketing plan. I'll do my best to give you feedback. For now, please make sure that you create, write down and save your own 3-sentence marketing plan.

The rest of this chapter will show you how to match "marketing buckets" to types of companies to help you get a sense of how to choose the strategies for your business.

Some of the common types of businesses are:

- Ecommerce (selling products)
- Agency type of business (selling services)
- Local service business
- Blogs
- New innovative start-ups
- Content on a platform business such as becoming a YouTuber or a podcaster
- Self-branded thought leader business
- Affiliate reseller
- B2B businesses

I broke down all kinds of businesses in the 9 above categories. This list covers about 95% of all businesses out there which makes it likely that one of these types of businesses is close to what your business is.

2. Marketing buckets

Categorizing different marketing strategies into marketing buckets helps you easily identify marketing strategies that might be right for your situation. Here is a list of general marketing buckets which together encompass almost all the possible marketing strategies you can choose from. Your job is to match the right marketing buckets to your business. I'll walk you through the matching process starting with the next section of this chapter. First, let's take a look at all the possible marketing buckets.

Naturally, they have some overlap between them because some are related. Also, they are implemented slightly differently when in different types of businesses so I'll describe them a little differently each time. But you should still see a logical pattern for how this all works together.

Here are the marketing buckets:

- Publicity - includes getting on the radio, podcasts, possibly TV, and being mentioned by big blogs or websites

- Discovery through search - leveraging SEO on Google and other big search engines like Amazon, YouTube, etc.

- Platform marketing - promoting a product on Amazon or eBay or YouTube or Udemy or iTunes or mobile app stores. This is all about mastering marketing on a specific platform.

- Long-term customer retention - if your customers love your business, it will be easier to sell to existing customers than finding new customers. The focus here is to make sure you have plenty of things to sell to your existing customers and that they get tremendous value from the initial products or services you sell them.

- Advertising - paying for promotion with Facebook ads, Google AdWords, YouTube AdWords, LinkedIn ads or ads elsewhere including offline mediums.

- B2B sales - having a direct sales staff that does outreach and makes sales.

- Local business marketing - a set of strategies used to promote local businesses like leveraging local search, business cards, fliers, etc. Local businesses are ones that serve clients within a certain radius, usually your immediate city. Some examples of local businesses are home repair, cleaning, dentist and medical offices, restaurants, stores and many other kinds of businesses.

- Event marketing - either creating your own event series or leveraging existing events.

- Referrals - establishing a referral network with other businesses and/or a customer referral program.

- Offline marketing - business networking with business cards, passing out fliers, door to door marketing and similar strategies.

- Quality and customer support - making sure your customers appreciate you so they remain long-term customers.

- Email marketing - good for customer retention and building an audience.

- Social media and virality - if your product or content is sharable in nature.

Now that you have a sense of what the marketing buckets are, in the following sections of this chapter I'll show you how to apply these marketing buckets to different kinds of businesses. The result will be a very solid second sentence of your three-sentence marketing plan. That's the sentence that has the ideal marketing strategies.

3. Marketing buckets for ecommerce business

Almost all ecommerce businesses either sell products from their own websites or large ecommerce platforms like Amazon, Etsy or eBay.

The ideal marketing strategy for ecommerce businesses is to leverage search. When people want certain products, they search for those products online. People who find your products while searching are typically very strong leads that tend to convert into paying customers better than people coming from other sources of traffic because they need little selling or convincing since they are already seeking out the kind of product you are selling. Your job is to make sure that they find your product when they search, and not the products of your competitors. If they find your products, you will have a high chance of making the sale.

The next bucket that will be an effective marketing strategy for an ecommerce business is platform marketing. By platform, I mean websites like Amazon, Etsy or whatever big ecommerce website is appropriate for the kind of product you are selling. If your product can become one of the top-selling products in its product category, you can get a flood of *consistent* sales.

Product quality is also a big marketing strategy because good products get recommended and customers leave nice reviews on them, further perpetuating the online word of mouth spread. It is also ethical to provide a high-quality product to someone who paid money for it.

Advertising (paying for promotion) is also a potentially viable promotion strategy in ecommerce. Advertising isn't for all products. For example, if your product doesn't have a high-profit margin, you don't have much money to spend on ads. You have to make sure that you are making more profit per sale than the cost of your products if you are to do advertising in a profitable and sustainable way.

Those are the top strategies to sell products. There are many other strategies to sell products, but pound for pound all the next strategies tend to be less effective.

Email marketing is also a fine way to promote products because you can build and grow an audience with your email marketing. When marketers are able to properly engage their email marketing audience, they are usually able to effectively sell products to them.

Additional strategies that might be effective to sell products are publicity and viral social sharing if the product is very unique, visual or exciting.

Notice that Facebook or Twitter marketing wasn't listed here. If your product is an ecommerce product, you probably thought Facebook marketing would be one of your main marketing strategies. Even though you can sell products on Facebook (I do so myself), the strategies above are usually much more effective at generating sales. In terms of actual effectiveness, unless your product is in the top 1% of virality for products, Facebook marketing doesn't even make the cut for ecommerce businesses.

4. Marketing buckets for agency business (selling services)

An agency business might be a software development agency, design agency, marketing agency, freelancing, copywriting, etc.

Again, the best types of clients will come from search because they are already looking for the services you are offering. Most agency businesses can help clients no matter where in the world their clients are located. But it is often easier to get ahead with SEO by doing local SEO and other local marketing.

Additional buckets that work for agencies are:

- Providing basic free/discounted services in an effort to upsell more services to clients and grow the lifetime customer value per client

- Content marketing and free tutorials for lead generation

- Email marketing

- Influencer marketing where the CEO or one of the main marketers in the company is positioned as a thought leader in the industry

- Professional and customer referral programs

5. Marketing buckets for a local business

Local businesses are businesses that serve clients within a local radius. That radius can be a five-block radius if the business is a liquor store or it can be a 100-mile radius if the business is a construction company, and you are willing to drive that far to construction sites.

Local businesses range from restaurants to home repair to stores to dentists and medical offices to mechanics and many other businesses. Surprisingly, the marketing strategies to promote local services are very similar from one seemingly different local business to another.

The main strategies to promote a local service business are:

- Local SEO through Google
- Customer and business referral program
- Marketing through local listings sites like yelp.com
- Local networking and business card marketing
- Storefront marketing
- Product quality
- Customer retention
- Ads like Google AdWords ads, Yelp.com ads or Facebook ads

For some local businesses, events or flier marketing can be additional options.

6. Marketing buckets for a blog

Blog marketing strategies are some of the most straightforward of all businesses. Here are the common marketing strategies for a blog:

- SEO for every blog post
- Social sharing for every blog post
- Customer retention to get people reading more of your content
- Differentiation and niche
- Authority building
- Quality
- Email marketing

7. Marketing buckets for an innovative website or start-up

Now that we covered how to promote a blog, which is a very basic website with just content, let's go over how to promote more complex websites. These can be websites like Airbnb or new social media sites.

The biggest challenge in promoting such websites is that since they are innovative and new, we are in uncharted territory at every step of the way.

Ecommerce websites, blogs or local businesses are generally proven businesses with proven business models and known marketing strategies. New start-ups are the exact opposite. Almost nothing is proven, and you have to carve out your own path. With that in mind, let's go over the marketing strategies for a new tech start-up.

- SEO
- Publicity due to the innovativeness and uniqueness of the business
- Sharing and friend invites

- Email marketing and long-term customer retention strategies

- Authority building

- Quality through rapid prototyping and customer feedback loop

Since many parts of your innovative business are unknown, your business model will constantly evolve. Since different parts of your original business idea will undergo many changes, every time the business model changes, your job is to also consider whether changes in the business model will open new marketing strategies or close existing ones.

For example, if you decide to stop being customer-facing (B2C) and become business-facing (B2B), strategies like social sharing and virality will be less of an option for you, but direct sales will become more of an option. Tweak your business model in a way that positions your business to have more natural marketing strategies.

8. Marketing buckets for platform marketing

What I refer to as platforms are very big sites on which you can build a very lucrative business. Some examples of such sites are Amazon.com, Udemy.com, YouTube.com, eBay.com, Etsy.com, podcasting on iTunes, mobile app stores like Apple App Store and Google Play Store, and many others. Here are the marketing strategies you must master to succeed in platform marketing.

- On-platform SEO (instead of Google search, this is search within the website on which you are doing business)

- Platform recommendation algorithm

- Creating highly attractive and highly converting listings of your products or content

- Product quality

- Long-term customer engagement

- Differentiation and uniqueness since on the platform you are competing with many similar offers

- Authority building

9. Marketing buckets for a thought leader business

A thought leader business is often a single person business where you position yourself as an expert in some niche or business area. Once you position yourself as an expert in something, you can consult, coach or train others within your area of expertise.

Here are some of the top marketing strategies for such a business:

- Content marketing - creating tutorials or other content in the area of your expertise and doing SEO for that content

- Hyper quality - since a thought leader is one of the very best in their niche or industry, everything you do must position you as such

- Social sharing, virality, and recommendations

- Long-term customer retention strategies

- Email marketing

- Choosing a niche and differentiation

- Community and fan/follower building

10. Marketing buckets for an affiliate business

Affiliate marketing has been around almost as long as marketing itself. At its core, it is just the act of reselling another person's or company's product or service for a commission. What's unique about affiliate marketing is that it has become very popular online.

Physical products are typically competitively priced, and there isn't enough profit in them for the manufacturer to be able to give a large commission to the reseller. Digital products, on the other hand, have no cost to reproduce after they have been created. This means that the manufacturer can give as much as a 90% commission, and still have the remaining 10% be pure profit, making it very lucrative for resellers to sell online products and services.

Typical marketing buckets for affiliate marketing are:

- SEO
- Ads
- Content marketing
- Email marketing

11. Marketing buckets for a b2b business

Businesses that have other businesses or organizations as clients have promotion strategies that fit into the following buckets.

- Direct sales and outreach
- Publicity to ensure that everyone in the industry who needs to know about them learns about them
- Carefully choosing a niche or business segment so that their publicity efforts are concentrated and they create a great product for that niche
- Long-term customer retention strategies
- SEO for some B2B companies. Usefulness of SEO can vary greatly from one specific product to another

12. Let's fix your 3-sentence marketing plan

Now comes the fun part. Using the matching of company types to marketing buckets, create a new 3-sentence marketing plan.

The first and third sentences of your marketing plan should remain the same. For most readers of this book, the second sentence should change drastically.

For a fun experiment, feel welcome to send me the original and revised versions of your 3-sentence marketing plan. I'll be glad to give you my honest feedback to make sure that you are on the right track.

My personal email address is:

alex.genadinik@gmail.com

My only request is that you keep both of your marketing plans at 3 sentences each. I get bombarded with email, and it would make it much easier to respond in a timely manner if your email wasn't too long. It would make it even easier for me if you titled your email something like "3-sentence marketing plan." I look forward to seeing your awesome plans.

CHAPTER 3: MARKETING PLAN SECTIONS & HOW TO THINK ABOUT THEM PRACTICALLY

"Do what you can, with what you have, where you are."

- Theodore Roosevelt

This chapter will give you brief introductions to other sections of the marketing plan and guide you on how to start thinking about them. This will give you the tools to then expand the 3-sentence marketing plan into a 1-page marketing plan, and we'll create your 1-page marketing plan in the following chapter.

1. Executive summary and company introduction

An executive summary is a brief introduction to the marketing plan. You can think of it as giving the reader a glimpse of what is to come. You can be general about what's coming up in the marketing plan because you will have a chance to be specific later in the document. Your goal is to get the reader interested enough in the marketing plan to move forward.

2. Company mission statement

The mission statement (sometimes called the mantra) is something that never changes. Strategy to achieve the mission statement always changes, but the mission statement itself does not change.

For example, a company's mission statement may be to "feed the hungry." That will always be the goal of the company, but the company might try to feed the hungry by buying up and distributing food or gathering donations for the hungry or finding access to cheaper food.

3. Goals, deadlines, and timelines

A professional marketing plan document should start with goals. After all, if you are at point A and you don't have a point B to get to, then you don't need a plan. All businesses have marketing goals. A goal may be to get to a certain level of traffic per day, per month or in total. It can also be to get a certain number of paying clients.

Once you set your goals, you should also give yourself a reasonable deadline to achieve those goals. It also helps to have additional, intermediate goals along your general timeline to help you stay on track.

4. Products and services being promoted

In this section, you describe the products and services that will be promoted. This shouldn't be a long section because most readers of this document will be well aware of which products and services are being promoted. Yet it is helpful to have this section to define the scope of the products and services being promoted.

5. Budget and resources

If you had an unlimited marketing budget, you could pursue every marketing strategy known to man. Since no company has an unlimited marketing budget, you must match the number of strategies you choose to your available resources. Resources can be cash, man-hours, assets (like an existing email list or website which you can use to promote things), or marketing partnerships.

6. Differentiation: how your business is unique

Even though differentiation and your unique value proposition (UVP) is always important, it can be argued that differentiation carries extra importance if your company is just being planned or is very young.

When you start a business, you almost never create a new market so most of the time you enter as a new player in an existing market. That means that on day one, your competitors are probably better than you and are more established. Over time you surely have a vision for how your company will be better and more established, but on day one you are the new kid on the block, and that is an inevitable reality.

Since there are established players in your market who are generally better than your new business, what you need in order to stand out is a compelling unique value proposition (UVP) that sets you apart.

You must position your business to be unique and different enough from existing competition. Maybe there is something that your competitors are not doing too well, and you can jump in and fill that void in the market. Or maybe your UVP can be something unique that you as the founder inherently bring with your approach. For example, you might be the top chef of certain cuisine and that can set you apart from competition if you open a restaurant. For other kinds of businesses, you might have the best designers on your team or the best engineers or the best customer service or a very unique and innovative way about how you deliver some solution.

Your UVP should ideally be identified during the planning stages of your business. You should also change, adjust and calibrate your UVP as your business starts and grows to eventually hone in on an ideal UVP that resonates with your potential customers, makes you stand out, and positions your business to dominate in your niche long-term.

Ultimately, your business should be unique and compelling in many ways. The more unique and compelling it is, the more customers and media attention it will attract.

7. Pricing and discounting strategies

Did you notice that some companies always seem to have ongoing sales or promotions? That is because sales and promotions help to create great headlines that make ads that convert. Discounts get people excited about going shopping since they will be getting a good deal. You should have a sales and promotions strategy too.

Think of what kind of promotions and discounts you can regularly run, and include them as a part of your marketing plan. They will give you more new ways to promote, more new customers, and give your previous customers a reason to shop with your business again.

8. Your target market

When new marketers or first-time business owners are asked about who their target customer is, they usually say something like "everyone" or "all men" or "all women" or all of some other gigantic un-targeted group.

While it is understood that you will take anyone as a customer, there are some people who are well suited to be your customers than most other people. You must identify who those people are so that you can craft a marketing strategy to reach as many such people as possible.

An ideal customer is a person who is experiencing the kind of problem that your business solves. They will covet and desire your solution much more than a random person.

You can identify potential customers by two things: demographics and psychographics.

Demographics are things that can be precisely measured. Examples of demographics are people's age, sex, income level, education level, marital status, parental status, whether they own a car or a house, geolocation, and many other things that can be quantified.

Psycho-graphics are attributes that can't be measured precisely but are still important. These are things like a person's motivations, desires, wants, hopes, fears, hobbies, interests, insecurities, mental blocks, emotions they are prone to, and even things like confusion and delusion.

Let me give you a concrete example of how I identify the target market for one of my products, which is this free Android business planning mobile app for entrepreneurs:

https://play.google.com/store/apps/details?id=com.problemio.two&hl=en_US

One of the most important and easiest to understand demographics for an app is geographic targeting. The app is an English-only app so the best countries for this app are countries where there is a large base of English speakers and Android users. These countries are USA, Canada, UK (I realize the UK isn't strictly a country), Australia, South Africa, India, and a few other large countries that have large populations because even if a small percentage of people in those countries speak English, that would still make for a significant user base of English speakers.

Other demographics for this app are more nuanced. Most people who use apps are generally younger. Most of the entrepreneurs on my app are first-time entrepreneurs. First-time entrepreneurs are generally younger. Most of the users for this app are under 30 years old, and often under 25 years old. Many of them are teenagers. They are usually not wealthy since usually younger people are less affluent than older people, and entrepreneurs are not known to be wealthy when they first start out either.

The psycho-graphics are where things get interesting. What are my users like as people? What do they need and want in life? Over time I have gotten to know my app users pretty well. Very often they aren't necessarily interested in starting a business as much as just needing to make some money in some way. Usually, that happens to people when they are in somewhat dire and stressful situations in life. They sometimes just need a little bit of direction because they usually have none or very little support in their business ventures or careers, and are generally very thankful when the app provides some support to them. Most of the businesses started on my apps start are not too technical. Most of the businesses being planned on my app are different kinds of local services.

By combining the demographics and psychographics of our customers we can get to know a lot about them. Once we have a deep understanding of our target customers, we can create a product that pleases them, and we can better understand how to promote the product to reach more similar people who are our target market.

9. How to identify your target market

When I first built my app, I didn't know any of the things that I know about my target customers now. I had other assumptions about them that proved to be wrong.

Originally, I thought that most of my app users were going to be geeky tech start-up entrepreneurs like the ones in Silicon Valley trying to make the next Facebook or Twitter. But that assumption was wrong. How did I ultimately learn what my app users really wanted, needed, were trying to do, and ultimately the kind of help they most needed? I talked to them.

In fact, over the years I have probably talked to between 2,000-3,000 of my app users! That is a crazy number, but I had to do it. Precisely from those conversations I learned what they needed the most, and I was able to improve the app to provide exactly that. Instead of assuming anything about them, I had them explain to me what they needed, which of their needs the app was meeting, and which needs the app wasn't meeting.

While I was having these conversations, I kept working on improving the app and making it more helpful to the app users based on insights that I got from having conversations with them.

This is what you have to do as well. You may start with certain assumptions about your customers, but you have to seek out your current customers and people who you assume are best suited to be your customers, talk to them, and get their insights.

This isn't just my advice. This approach is an industry-standard. Find ways to engage your current and potential customers in conversation, and listen to their thoughts closely. You don't have to take everyone's advice, but you should try to definitely understand the nature of their experience and learn how it can be improved.

10. Target market definitions

Serviceable market - part of the total addressable market targeted by your products.

Total addressable market - total revenue available in the marketplace. For example, the entire small business industry.

Realistically attainable market - the market portion that can be realistically reached.

Serviceable market - part of the total addressable market targeted by your products.

Total addressable market - total revenue available in the marketplace. For example, the entire small business industry.

11. Building a customer avatar

To understand even more about your ideal customers, some people like to create an "avatar" of an ideal customer. This is a fancy term for outlining some of the key traits of a target customer and imagining a day in their life.

An avatar is a description of a fictitious potential customer. It helps you better understand the needs of your customers. It also helps you understand when during their day they might discover or consume your product, when they are most ready to buy, and what they need from your product.

Your avatar should resemble a real person as closely as possible, starting with giving them a real name. I'll give you an example of an avatar for a user of my apps.

Let's call this Avatar Steve (don't ask me why I chose this name). Steve lives in Ohio. He still lives at home. He is in his second year of college. He is bored of college and he is bored with his part-time job. In fact, as many other young people working basic jobs, he hates working at his part-time job, and he is not looking forward to getting a boring corporate job when he gets out of college. Steve spends much of his free time daydreaming and trying to figure out a different path for his life. In his idle time at work or college, he sometimes looks for apps, online tools or YouTube videos about entrepreneurship. Sometimes he talks to his peers about starting a business. His friends might be eager to explore business ideas with him, but none of them have any experience or know what kind of a business is good for them to get into or how to pull it off even if they do open that business.

At some point, maybe when he is extra bored or on his break, Steve can discover my app when he is looking for tools to help him figure out what business to get into and how to pull it off. Steve might also discover the app when looking for slightly more concrete help once he gets some business ideas that he is interested in pursuing. The reason he would discover an app and not a website is because he is on break from work or at school so he can only search on his phone which increases the likelihood of him looking for apps.

As an exercise, try to create a few different customer avatars for your business. It should help you understand how to make a product that delights your customers, and how to market it.

12. Branding strategy

Branding can be a confusing term because it is often used to mean a few different things. Let's put a few of them in perspective. The first way to look at branding is consistency of the look and feel of all your marketing materials from your website to your logo to every other visual component of your business. Another way to look at branding is to ask yourself "how do customers perceive my business?" and "how do I want them to view my business?" Another way to understand branding is to look at it as recognition. A brand is something that is recognized in your industry by peers and customers.

That segues well to one of my favorite branding strategies, which is all about making your business and your personal brand stand out as a thought leader, and gain authority and respect within your industry.

The branding of the look and feel of your business is commoditized and relatively straightforward. All the designs and the logo have to have repeating colors and a consistent look and feel. Whoever designs your logo and website will help you with that.

The more challenging part of your branding is to get many people to actually come across your branding in one way or another, and then remember it in a positive way after having a positive experience with your business.

For people to actually see your branding, you either have to do a lot of marketing, or do something noteworthy and stand out so that more people can take notice of your business.

One great way that I like to build my personal and company brand is to create a very big platform for myself. Let me explain what I mean by that. Many well-known people become well-known (you can think about it as being well branded) by creating something big like writing a *popular* book, hosting a *popular* podcast or a YouTube show, or creating a *highly read* blog, or something else that became popular. These big things that people create serve as a platform for the individuals or their companies to gain notoriety, and improve their branding by becoming a trusted authority in their industry.

13. Competitive analysis

In this section of a marketing plan you must take a close look at who your competitors are, and create a strategy for how you will out-compete them.

Some common ways to beat your competition is to offer a better product, be better at marketing, think of new and innovative marketing tactics, brand yourself or your business as more of an authority in your business niche, or adjust your company's unique value proposition (UVP again) to be more interesting and attractive to potential customers.

14. Customer retention strategy

The customer retention section is one of my personal favorite parts of creating any kind of marketing strategy.

New marketers are usually most excited to hunt for new customers, and I love that hunt too. But what many first-time marketers don't realize is that it is often easier to sell to an existing customer than to find a new customer. In fact, one of the panaceas of business is to get a customer that shops with your business regularly by either becoming a subscriber or regularly consuming something your business offers.

Let me give you a number of suggestions for what you can do to retain customers longer, and have them buy more from your business over time. If you succeed at this, customers might generate thousands of percent more profit for you over time! A customer who buys from you once a month every month generates 1200% more revenue in a year than a customer who buys just once.

One of the most common ways to retain your customers is, of course, by providing a good product or service. I have to keep harping on the issue of quality because it is so important, and often neglected by first-time entrepreneurs. A good product makes your customers trust you. On the other hand, if a customer has a bad experience with your product, they will never buy anything from you again.

Another way to retain your customers is through email marketing. You can create a regular newsletter that delivers value and insight to your customers. By providing value, you will make them appreciate your business. You can sometimes also send offers and discounts in your email newsletter (not too often so that the people getting these emails don't get too annoyed).

Another way to retain your customers is by creating multiple products or services that your customers can buy. If your customers are happy with the first product they bought, they might buy a second and a third item from you.

Personally, I like to be able to present many products (a catalog) to people. This is why I created many online courses, many apps, and wrote many books. If a person likes any of these, they can get more. It works in combination with product quality. If people appreciate your work, they are likely to want more of it, and having multiple products allows you to offer them just that. Offering multiple great products is great for your customers and it is great for you.

Another long-term customer retention strategy is to offer products or services that you can sell either on a subscription basis or that are consumed and needed by your customers on a regular basis. These are sometimes called consumables. Offering consumables is kind of like offering a subscription because customers consume them regularly without the customer feeling like they are getting locked into something which is how subscriptions can sometimes make people feel.

Subscriptions are great because when people sign up for them, they don't have to make the purchasing decision every time. Some people even forget to unsubscribe while not even using the service. A great example of that is a gym membership. Think of how many people out there have a regular gym membership for which they pay monthly, but never even go to the gym. It requires time and effort to unsubscribe, whereas if a person is not subscribed, it takes an effort to buy again, which is a deterrent.

For you, the challenge is to come up with products or services that fit the consumable or subscription model. Those revenue streams are not an ideal fit for every product or business. It can take some massaging of your overall business model in order for various long-term customer retention strategies to become a natural fit in how you operate your overall business.

15. Strategy to maximize referrals

When first-time marketers tell me that old phrase that they will promote their business with "Facebook, Twitter, business cards and fliers" sometimes at the end they add "and get referrals." What they don't realize is that there are a few kinds of referrals. I'll break down each type and how to optimize for them.

I often talk about 3 different ways to get referrals.

- Customer referrals

- Referrals from other businesses

- Incentivized referrals (with a commission)

Let's start with how to get referrals from your existing customers, and get your current customers to invite their friends. This is what some people sometimes refer to as word of mouth marketing.

The most important thing in boosting customer referrals is your product quality (sorry to sound like a broken record on the quality issue). If your product or service is amazing and leaves your customers thrilled and feeling like they just got an amazing value, they will naturally talk about your product or service with friends and recommend it.

But even if your customers truly love your product or service, they are too busy with their lives to go around promoting your product all day. They won't recommend it to their friends as often as you would like. There just isn't enough for them in it. For that reason, whenever possible, you must give them incentives, and the incentives must be for the current customer *and* any new potential customers they might invite.

For example, if you offer an existing customer 20% OFF their next purchase if they bring a friend, there is not enough incentive for the friend to try your business. And if you only give 20% OFF to the friend, there is not enough incentive for the current customer. But if you give 20% OFF (or whatever other discount) to each of them, then suddenly the current customer will have enough incentive to invite friends, and the friends will know that they will be getting a good deal, and will come more readily.

This is how you boost social referrals: through very high-quality services and products, and double incentives. Don't just rely on people to recommend your business to others. Control, influence, and maximize referrals with correct incentives.

Another way to get referrals is to get professional referrals by partnering with other companies. This strategy is completely different from getting customer referrals. To get professional referrals, you need to build relationships with similar but not exactly the same businesses as yours which can refer clients to you and you can refer clients to them.

For example, the medical community has this nailed down pat. If you go to a general physician and he spots a skin problem, he recommends you to go see a skincare doctor (dermatologist). If you have a foot problem, he recommends a foot doctor (podiatrist). If he thinks some medicine can help you, he prescribes that medicine. Being on that doctor's recommendation list can drive a lot of businesses to other doctors.

You can consider doing something similar for your business. If you are a mechanic, build relationships with companies that clean cars, paint cars, sell and install fancy rims or car stereo systems, and so on. If their customers ever need a mechanic, they can refer those customers to you. And if your customers ever need a paint job or ask about car stereo systems, you can refer those people to your referral partners. This will create a professional network of companies who refer clients to one another and boost each other's businesses.

The third way you get professional referrals is by paying other companies for leads they send you, or paying a commission after one of the leads they send becomes a paying customer. Paying for leads is a very powerful way to incentivize other companies to send you referrals because money is a great motivator.

16. Content marketing strategy (free content)

This is an optional section. If your company's marketing is largely made up of online marketing, then it is advisable to have a content marketing section. Content marketing is all about giving away free content in order to make that content easier to promote. People jump on free offerings and by giving something away for free you can lure many people to your free content. Once they are in the middle of consuming your free content, you can promote your paid content to them.

Common examples of content marketing are blog posts, YouTube videos, and podcasts.

17. S.W.O.T analysis

S.W.O.T is an acronym. It stands for:

S - Strengths: these are your advantages and things that will help you be competitive and find success.

W - Weaknesses: every business has weaknesses, and it is important to be honest about them with yourself as a company. If you identify your weaknesses, you can either position your business to avoid those weaknesses or fix them.

O - Opportunities: opportunities are areas in the market that you might see as being underserved where you can fill in the gap or areas where your competitors are not doing a great job in.

T - Threats: threats can be competitors or bigger market fluctuations. For example, you might be in an unproven market or your business might be too risky for some reason.

Identifying these helps you create a stronger overall strategy.

18. KPI (key performance indicators)

Every business has elements that are vital for overall growth. You must identify what those elements are for your business, and work to make sure that they always do better and better. These are the key metrics for you to track.

Some of the most important metrics for every business are revenue and profit. But those metrics tend to go up only after other metrics go up before them.

For example, let's say that your business is a YouTube channel. It might seem that the important metric is revenue, and it is. But revenue goes up only after you increase other metrics like total minutes watched, average minutes watched per video, viewer engagement, and views.

Those metrics would be your KPIs (key performance indicators) that you identify as important for your business. The benefit of identifying your KPIs is that you can then focus your business strategy and allocate attention and resources to grow those KPIs, and with them, your business.

19. Outlining marketing strategies (practical example)

Since at the heart of your marketing plan are the actual marketing strategies, this is where the magic happens. To make it as practical as possible, I'll share how I do the high-level planning for marketing my successful online business so you can have takeaways to apply to your situation.

To tell you a little bit about my business, I have a number of products and services (apps, books, online courses, coaching) that help entrepreneurs plan, start and grow their businesses.

My biggest long-term goal is to brand myself as an expert. I am accomplishing that by putting a long-term effort into establishing myself as one of the biggest business experts on a few large platforms like Amazon, Udemy and YouTube.

Remember earlier in this book when I talked about branding yourself in a thought leader business by creating platforms for yourself so that you could stand out in your business niche? A great book or a great app can get you notoriety and position you as one of the leaders in your niche.

My niche is marketing and entrepreneurship. Here is what I did:

First, I created a large YouTube channel that focuses on business and marketing:

http://www.youtube.com/user/Okudjavavich

This channel has 2,000,000 views at the time of writing this book. I've moved on from YouTube and don't post many new videos, but I still get views and traffic from it regularly.

I also become a prominent online instructor teaching mainly business and marketing:

https://www.udemy.com/user/alexgenadinik

And as you can see from my instructor profile, I am also a 3-time bestselling Amazon author, writing business and marketing books.

I also created mobile apps on entrepreneurship which have a cumulative 2,000,000+ downloads at the time of this writing. Although, I have to admit that I've moved on from the app world and lost some excitement for it.

I've done other things, but even with these accomplishments, I've positioned myself in the 98th or 99th percentile of most people who try to do business online. This helps me increase sales across almost all my products and services because I have given myself big platforms to stand on and become authoritative in a few niches of focus.

The next thing I focus on as a part of my marketing is investing in my own personal education and improvement. This is similar to hiring more staff that have additional or improved skillsets. Improving my own skills also helps me make better products. If I teach myself to focus better or to improve my sales, I'll create better and more successful apps, books, videos and provide better coaching. Recall how I emphasize the importance of product quality throughout this book. Product is never perfect, and I always feel that I have a long way to go, and I am always thinking about how to improve my skills so I can create better products for my clients.

As an example, even this book is on its 3rd rewrite. Every year I improve my skills as a writer, notice how the book can be better and re-write the book. The book is never perfect, and every once in a while when I feel that I've gathered enough feedback and improved enough of my skills, I edit the book to make it better. I do my best to improve all my products over time.

My next marketing tactics are SEO and social media. Notice that my priorities are long-term, big vision things like branding, positioning and improving my skills for the future. Actual tactical marketing takes 3rd highest priority.

The reason I mention SEO and social media in the same proverbial breath is that they can work well together and amplify each other's effectiveness. For example, when I create a video on YouTube, I do a lot of SEO for that video to try to get it to rank higher in YouTube search. Once it ranks in Google search, many of the viewers share the video on social media and give it an extra boost, further strengthening the SEO and rankings of that video on YouTube.

When I create products like books, apps or online courses, part of the planning for them is to make sure that they are set up well to be discovered via search or whatever recommendation algorithms are prominent on the sites those products are on. If a book or other product idea doesn't lend itself well to being discovered through search, it is a sign that I shouldn't write it because a big marketing strategy won't be available to promote that product.

My marketing strategy is setup to combine some of the most powerful concepts in online marketing like great personal and business branding, SEO, video marketing, social media tactics, and platform marketing.

CHAPTER 4: 1-PAGE MARKETING PLAN

In this chapter, we'll take a 3-sentence marketing plan and expand it into a 1-page marketing plan using some of the sections from the previous chapter.

1. Chapter introduction and another 3-sentence marketing plan

Let's quickly create another 3-sentence marketing plan to reinforce what we learned earlier. Instead of a marketing plan for just my mobile apps, I'll make a 3-sentence marketing plan for my entire business.

If you have not sent me your 3-sentence marketing plan for feedback, you are still welcome to do that. Here is the 3-sentence marketing plan for my overall business.

Sentence 1: My business is a thought leader business in the business planning, business strategy, entrepreneurship and marketing spaces that's monetized through books, courses, apps, and coaching.

Sentence 2: My marketing strategies are platform marketing on

Amazon, Udemy and a few other platforms, product quality, long-term customer retention, and customer support.

Sentence 3: I differentiate from other thought leaders by choosing a few specific niches (business planning, strategy and scalable marketing), quality, and a strong eye towards customer care.

2. Turning the 3-sentence plan into a 1-page plan

If you are worried about moving up in planning difficulty, the good news is that three sentences are already about 15-20% of a page, and even more of the page will be taken up by section headings.

The most important question to answer when going from a 3-sentence plan to a 1-page plan is which additional sections should we now add from our choices in the previous chapter.

The marketing for each company is different, and different sections take priority depending on what's important for your situation. So you don't have to follow my suggestion precisely, but I suggest to add these sections as you expand from the 3-sentence plan to a 1-page plan:

- Spend a few sentences instead of one sentence on your marketing strategies
- Instead of having one sentence explaining your differentiation and niche, add a section discussing your competition and how you will be different
- Add a section about your target customer and target market and your niche
- If you have space left on the page, add a section about your long-term customer retention
- If you have space left on the page, add a section with your goals and budget

With these possible additions in mind, the next section will contain my 1-page marketing plan.

3. My 1-page marketing plan for a year

My business:

Thought leader and authority business in the entrepreneurship and marketing space.

Goals:

Steady, 5% month over month growth for my books and online course sales during the first 9 months of the year and more aggressive 10-20% growth during the last three months of the year, which is the traditional shopping season.

Marketing strategies:

- Product quality: I will spend extra time re-writing my books and re-filming my courses to make them the best products in their niches

- Focus on customer care and support to build superfans that leave nice reviews and buy more of my products

- Grow lead generation for my coaching

- Implement ad retargeting to my website visitors

- Implement social media automation on Twitter, Facebook, LinkedIn and Pinterest so I can be more hands-off there

- Experiment with advertising (paying for traffic) with Facebook ads to bring new traffic (whereas ad retargeting brings back past visitors)

- Spend time learning how to be a better presenter on video

Differentiation:

My goal this year is to stand out through the quality of my products and customer care. The strategy is that the quality of my work will boost my marketing efforts, and my products will climb in the rankings and recommendation algorithms on platforms where I sell them.

Target customer:

Ideal customers are people planning to start a business or people who have already started a business, and understand the value of good advice and guidance. Ideal customers are professionals who are consistent and won't quit their business at first sign of difficulties. If they are consistent in their effort, I'll be able to help them long-term with ongoing coaching and with multiple books and courses.

Competition:

I am obviously not the biggest thought leader in business. There are many giants in this space. That is why I focus on a few smaller business niches where I can be one of the top experts there like business planning, business strategy, mobile apps, and scalable marketing techniques.

4. Section conclusion

That was pretty simple, wasn't it? It might have been difficult to create a 1-page marketing plan from scratch, but because you already had the 3-sentence marketing plan written, it was a much simpler jump.

In the next chapter, we'll take your 1-page marketing plan, and expand it into a full, professional marketing plan.

CHAPTER 5: FIRST FULL MARKETING PLAN EXAMPLE

In this chapter, we will walk through the first example of a full marketing plan. The first is a marketing plan for a business that puts on large conferences in the information security industry. I chose that business because it is an entirely different type of business from the ones we've been discussing, and it will give us some fresh perspectives. In the next chapter, we'll expand the 1-page marketing plan for my business into a full marketing plan.

Marketing plan example

Business:

Large trade show and conference series in the information security industry.

Goals:

Our goal is to generate 30,000 email sign-ups and an attendance of 15,500+ professionals in the information security industry, and with that to become one of the largest annual conventions for this industry worldwide.

Another goal is to get 100+ exhibitors to purchase exhibition space at the event.

Unique Value Proposition:

This event represents the best chance to network with 15,000 peers and some of the leading experts in this industry from all over the world, learn from our top keynote speakers, and see which companies are making waves in this industry this year and beyond.

Deadlines:

Marketing plan agreement and finalization: 2 weeks

Marketing channels set-up: 1 month

Marketing channel growth: 12 months to the event deadline

Smaller events begin in 6 months and the large trade show begins in 14 months.

Budget:

Excluding salary, the spending budget is $100,000.

Budgeting marketing initiatives:

- Local event marketing: $2,000/month per city
- Ongoing email marketing and social media: $2,000/month
- Running a YouTube/podcast show: $1,000/month
- SEO strategy: $1,000/month
- Publicity: $1,000-$5,000/ month
- Ad (paid) Facebook, Twitter, YouTube and LinkedIn: $2,000 per month
- Miscellaneous and unforeseen costs: $2,000 per month

Total: $11,000 - $19,000 per month.

The ideal budget is in the $15,000/month range. That is higher than our $100,000 budget. Our plans currently exceed the budget due to pursuing local event groups and hiring a publicist, which are strategies that can be taken out of the marketing plan if the marketing budget does not increase.

Additional resources:

Unknown: extra staff may be needed.

Differentiation: how this event is unique and why people *must* attend it

This is the biggest Information Security convention and has the most professionals, high-level company officers, and CEOs of any other similar event.

The large convention is the annual event where the industry learns about the future of the industry, and the biggest names in the industry attend and present.

What will truly set this conference apart is the constant brand building and re-marketing within the industry via the accompanying podcast and YouTube show. The show will help our company's events be on the forefront of people's minds whenever they think of information security. The show will grow its audience over time, and position the company as a thought leader within the industry.

Additionally, our regular newsletter will provide valuable best-of-industry curated content from around the web, which will make this a great newsletter.

With the show and the insightful newsletter, this will become a respected brand known for delivering amazing value. This will make the marketing of the conference much simpler because the big event and the smaller ones throughout the year would provide more value than the regular show viewers and newsletter readers already get and enjoy.

On a more concrete note, with our publicity strategy, Google search and YouTube search SEO strategy, this conference will stand out as the best, most well-recognized event and conference series, and have more visibility than competitive conferences.

Target market who we are targeting:

This event is targeting Information Security industry professionals (engineers, business managers, and business owners) and companies that want to advertise to them.

Marketing strategies:

There will be a few components for the customer acquisition strategy. This section will list them all, go into more detail on each, and then tie in how all these strategies will work together to maximize one another.

1) Email marketing and making use of Infosecurity-magazine

Email marketing and magazine subscriptions will be the key long-term tactic to promote the conference. Email will allow us to regularly reach potential attendees and exhibitors with reminders about event dates and things to look forward to at the events.

Email is the most consistent way to reach and inform our potential audience. Once people are signed up for our email updates and newsletter, we will work on engaging them. We will send them updates every 2 weeks, and more frequently than that during the months immediately prior to an event.

If we are successful at engaging our email recipients, this will be the highest converting channel for us.

2) Google SEO strategy

We will also focus on Google SEO (search engine optimization). Here are the keywords we need to rank for that will get us potential attendees and exhibitors.

Keywords to target attendees: news in information security, information security, information security events, information security UK, information security Europe, information security conference, meet professionals in information security, and so on.

Keywords to target vendors to exhibit: same keywords as to target attendees AND choose a few types of main kinds of exhibitors, and for whatever they might be selling, see what they might search when researching how to get clients, and try to rank in Google for that.

While SEO is considered mainly a Google search strategy, we will also target these keywords with our YouTube videos.

3) Building our own publicity channels

Using social media to build your own large marketing channel(s) is the professional and effective way to use social media. We will establish a YouTube show on the latest and greatest in the Information Security industry, and take the audio from the YouTube show and turn it into a podcast.

We can make the podcast prominent in our industry, and easily become the top podcast for our industry because there aren't many podcasts that cover our industry.

We can do the same on YouTube.

The podcast/YouTube would be interview-based. We would strategically invite industry leaders to be interviewed, each of whom would already have a large following in the industry. They would help us drive traffic to our shows. Those new viewers and listeners would also sign up for our email newsletter subscriptions.

On YouTube and in iTunes (with the podcast) we would also rank for keywords like "Information Security" which are too competitive to rank in Google SEO.

4) Publicity from industry publication

Just like we would invite others to be guests on our show, we would get publicity and mentions on blogs, podcasts, YouTube shows, and magazines that cover our industry.

On those publicity spots, we would try to funnel people to subscribe to our shows, newsletter, or engage with us in other ways. This can be an inexpensive paid strategy because paying bloggers and podcasters to be on their shows can get us interviews and publicity ASAP.

5) Local events strategy

There are a few places in the world that are hubs for technology professionals. They are San Francisco Bay Area, New York, London, Berlin, and Tel Aviv.

We can hire part-time event planners in each of those cities to build weekly (this is aggressive because we don't have too much time before the conference. Usually it would be by-weekly or monthly) events in those cities. Attendees would register with their email addresses, and we would be able to send them reminders of the conference.

Additionally, during those local events, the organizer can talk about the sponsor for those events (the conference is the sponsor) and encourage the attendees to get their companies to attend and present there as vendors and not just as regular attendees.

We can promote those local events on meetup.com, other local event websites, and in partnership with local information security companies who will present at those events. We can also network with other, more established events to co-host events to get some of their audience to learn about our conference.

6) Social media marketing strategy

Effective social media marketing strategies are outlined above. Additional basic strategies would be to have a Twitter account, Facebook (group and a page on Facebook as they each have different functions) pages from which to get people to follow and like, and update them on the latest discounts and exciting things that will happen at the conference.

7) Paid strategy (advertising)

Google AdWords, YouTube AdWords, Facebook, Twitter, and LinkedIn are also good places to run paid advertising campaigns to target professionals in the Information Security industry, and we will experiment with all of these options.

Strategy to maximize customer referrals:

Attendees are most excited about the event when they register. At that point, they are the most enthusiastic and engaged in thinking about the event. This is a great time to ask them to invite other industry professionals who might also like the conference. We will give them and their friends discounts if their friends attend.

Strategy to maximize business referrals:

Since most revenue will come from exhibitors, the main strategy to get those customers will be to give a discount to an exhibitor who refers any additional exhibitor, and give both of them a discount so that both of them are incentivized.

Customer retention strategy:

Regular content like email newsletters, Twitter and Facebook updates, and a YouTube/podcast show are all mechanisms to drive consistent and regular engagement.

These strategies will retain attendees for this year's conference, and will truly reach their full potential as they get established as authoritative voices in the coming years.

CHAPTER 6: SECOND FULL MARKETING PLAN EXAMPLE

In this chapter, I'll go over the marketing plan for my thought leadership and self-branding business.

Disclaimer: Please don't take the examples of my own company as me promoting the company. I give these examples because I have the most real insight about it - not to promote it.

Introduction and executive summary:

The business is a self-branded business that focuses on positioning Alex Genadinik as a thought leader in entrepreneurship and uses his online brand recognition to stand out on the web, build trust, and sell products and services that help people plan, start and grow their businesses.

Products:

The company offers products for entrepreneurs across different mediums, offering books, video-based products, and mobile apps. The quality of the products is one of the best marketing strategies for this business because if people like the products, they will buy more of them, and recommend them to friends, and the company has multiple products entrepreneurs can consume in every medium. If one person likes one book, the business offers 19 more books for them to try.

Through quality, the company is able to increase revenue many-fold.

- 20 business and marketing books on Amazon
- 100+ courses on Udemy
- 800+ free videos on YouTube
- 4 unique mobile apps on Android and iPhone
- Affiliate product sales for web hosting

Services:

While the business sells services, these services are largely a way to create business relationships and generate leads for products because this business is mostly a product-based business.

- Full multi-week coaching programs
- Hourly coaching
- Freelancing
- SEO services

Free content (content marketing strategy):

The company uses free content to help new potential clients see the value and level of insight they will be getting from the premium products. It is a way to sell premium products and services. The free content is also a way to give great support to existing clients to make them happier with their purchases.

- YouTube
- Blog content
- Live with periscope
- Live on YouTube Live
- Google Hangouts with Udemy students

[To the reader: notice that the paid content is also a content marketing strategy. Many people think that a content marketing strategy needs to have free content that you use to upsell your paid content. But it doesn't have to be that way. Your paid content can also promote your other content.]

Major Goals (12 months deadline):

1. 5% month over month growth in Udemy students in the first 8 months of the year and 10% month over month growth for the last 4 months of the year

2. 25% year over year sales growth on books

3. 10% annual growth in views on YouTube (I have shifted focus away from YouTube since it doesn't have large financial returns

4. 10% annual growth in app downloads (I have also shifted focus away from my apps)

5. At least small growth rate for my coaching lead generation

6. At least a small growth rate in traffic for my website problemio.com

7. Identify, research and start work on an additional platform

8. Improve branding

9. Grow Clarity.fm presence

[To the reader: notice that I switched focus to branding channels that are also direct commerce channels. I have shifted focus to growing my course sales on Udemy and my books on Amazon, and deprioritized everything else by setting very small growth rated for things like YouTube or apps.]

Budget & Resources:

- I have a $3,000/month budget for hiring and running ads that barely gets used.

- I spend 30 hours per week on marketing.

45

- Looking to hire marketing and advertising help in the form of either one full-time employee or a few effective part-time consultants.

Differentiation & Unique Value Proposition:

My approach is different because:

1. Products and services come from a deep knowledge of the business areas I cover, customer experience, needs, and true care about the success of my customers
2. Out-market most of my competition
3. Brand growth and recognition
4. Proven track record of my own business
5. Affordable pricing
6. Value
7. Trust
8. Catalog approach in being able to offer multiple products
9. Relentless work ethic
10. A fun and not too formal approach
11. Responsiveness and customer support
12. Apps that make my business stand out since it is still an exciting space

Pricing, Discounts and Sale Strategies:

1. I use the Freemium business model with my apps and content marketing. By giving away free content, I up-sell my paid products.
2. Monthly promotions with heavy discounts on my Udemy courses
3. Free quarterly book promotions
4. General pricing is aimed to give value

5. Catalog approach where I position many affordable products next to one another to allow people to afford more than one

Market demographics:

- 60% men and 40% women
- 40% US, 8% UK, 6% Canada, 4% Australia, 3% India, 3% South Africa, 3% Malasia, 3% Indonesia, 1% Israel. Other customers come from the rest of the world.
- Mostly unemployed
- Mostly poor
- 15% employed, looking to start their business. These are ideal because they are able to spend most
- 15% existing small businesses that also have a budget for spending
- Mostly 18-35 and 50+
- Mostly single
- Mostly low education
- Mostly sparse work experience

Market psychographics:

- Hate their job
- Struggling to find a career
- Struggling financially
- Anxiety
- Need money now
- Need help now
- Can't afford too much
- Pressure from society, family
- Focus issues

- Poor professionals
- Forced to be creative, outside the box
- Don't execute well
- Low confidence, uncertainty

Customer avatar:

We will name him Joe. Joe has a part-time job, but he doesn't like it because it doesn't challenge him and it isn't fulfilling. Plus, his boss isn't nice. Joe has no idea how to get out of it. He hears other people around him talk about starting a business or making money online, and it feels like an ideal way for him to get out of his current situation.

One day after an especially bad workday, he takes action. He goes online and searches Google for what kind of online business he can start. After some surfing, he learns that he can start a blog or an affiliate business without having any products and with minimal costs. This is where his journey starts.

Over time, he struggles, fails, but if he keeps trying, he will listen to podcasts, try apps, watch YouTube videos, and hire freelancers or coaches to help him do better with his business. He can discover my business at any of these points.

Market needs:

Since this market is saturated with low-quality coaches and low-quality informational products, the biggest market need is quality and real guidance. Entrepreneurs need fast and effective strategies to succeed with their businesses.

In one sentence, here is what entrepreneurs need:

Credible, quality, and effective advice that will move them forward in their business.

Market trends:

This is a growing market. As in any growing market, with growth comes an increase in competition. With increased competition comes consolidation which is when struggling competitors die off. We have not yet hit the point of saturation and consolidation, but there is an increase of competition across the board whether I am selling apps, books, online courses, YouTube videos, or consulting services.

This market is rapidly growing and also becoming increasingly competitive.

Another trend is that video content consumption is rapidly growing, and text consumption is decreasing, especially among the younger generation.

Another trend is that most entrepreneurs want things done for them instead of learning.

Market growth:

Here is an article for reference:

https://elearningindustry.com/elearning-statistics-and-facts-for-2015

Statistics from the article:

The global eLearning Market is expected to reach $107 billion by 2015 [5]. The global self-paced eLearning market reached $32.1 billion in revenue in 2010 [3], with a five year compound annual growth rate of approximately 9.2%. This means that the self-paced eLearning market should see estimated revenues of $49.9 billion in 2015 [3].

Highest growth by country:

1. India: 55%
2. China: 52%
3. Malaysia: 41%

4. Romania: 38%
5. Poland: 28%
6. Czech Republic: 27%
7. Brazil: 26%
8. Indonesia: 25%
9. Colombia: 20%
10. Ukraine: 20%

Additionally, corporate training is projected to grow by 13% by 2017.

SWOT (strengths, weaknesses, opportunities, threats):

Strengths:

- Very hands-on and credible
- Growing authority
- Very good at marketing
- Growing relationships

Weaknesses:

- Single person business
- Financially risk-averse

Opportunities:

- Still young elearning market
- Live coaching
- New social media channels
- Boost website traffic
- Grow on Amazon and Udemy

Threats:

- Competition
- Changes in online space

Branding Strategy:

Brand everything as Alex Genadinik (unique name) and bright photo with blue background that you see on my YouTube, Udemy and other website profiles.

Focus on my unique name, and brand myself as an expert. The brand is myself and the goal is to make me recognized as someone who is expert at what they do and provides good value for customers and goes above and beyond for them.

Reinforce expertise with large traffic and sale numbers to build extra recognition.

Competitive Analysis:

Some competitive self-branded experts in my business niches are:

Nick Loper from SideHustleNation.com - main approach is podcasting, book publishing, and masterminds

John Dumas from Entrepreneur on Fire podcast - the main approach is podcasting and selling training not on Udemy

Me: YouTube, books, apps, and Udemy instead of a podcast

I compete on many platforms below, and my competition is very fragmented. I differentiate myself with quality and customer care as a theme on all platforms:

- Amazon - Books on topics I researched deeply or have done successfully myself
- Udemy - Complete suite of nearly every topic in starting a business

- Mobile apps - quality and helpfulness
- Coaching - based on trust, clients come from my existing marketing channels

Customer Retention Strategy:

- Get customer contact information like email addresses to let them know of monthly discounts and promotions
- Create products that should be used one after another in a sequence
- Have regularly published content so that people know to come back on a regular basis and get value
- Email marketing
- Make repeat-use products
- Add a subscription service
- Create a catalog of products to allow people who enjoy my products to get more than one and get further help from them

Maximizing Business Referrals:

I will find similar businesses in my field, and:

- Give them financial incentives (commissions) to recommend my business
- Or promote their business to my customers in return
- Do this with as many businesses as possible without stretching yourself or spamming your customers

Maximizing Customer/Social Referrals:

- Make my apps better if used with friends. I added features to my apps that can be used with business partners
- Give friend AND existing customer discount to incentivize them

- Focus on making customers into super fans by giving them amazing customer support and build great products for them

Key Performance Indicators (KPI):

Things I will track, often with analytics software.

Example YouTube:

- # of views
- growth of views from month to month
- # of minutes watches per view
- revenue

Example for my website:

- Overall traffic
- Search traffic
- Social media traffic (each channel)
- Time on site growing
- Revenue and sales

Example for a sales platform like Amazon:

- Daily sales
- Weekly trends
- Year over year trends
- Readership per book, especially after rewriting a book (you can track this with Kindle Unlimited readers)

Sales plan:

- Hiring cold callers for business research and outreach
- SEO for important B2B lead keywords
- Books as specific lead generation

Advertising plan:

- A small investment in Facebook ads
- A small investment in AdWords ads
- A small investment in YouTube video ads
- A small investment in local Yelp ads

Financial objectives (NOT REAL FINANCIAL DATA):

- Udemy sales: $75,000
- Amazon sales: $30,000
- B2B sales: $25,000
- Coaching: $10,000
- Ads: $4,000
- Affiliate: $5,000

Total: $149,000

Fixed costs (monthly)

- Social media automation software $25
- Publicity community $7
- Hiring $500
- Advertising $600
- Coaching/learning on how to create better products: $300

Total: $1,433 / month

Annual expense forecast: $17,196

If I can meet revenue projections, I can raise the marketing expense budget (monthly)

- Additional equipment: $100
- Additional SEO: $200
- Development: $300
- Freelancers: $500

Break-even analysis (optional):

Count total business expenses and create realistic marketing and revenue projections to meet your spending. That is a breakeven point. The breakeven point is a very important point for new businesses because once you reach that, you know you won't go out of business, and you can begin making more wiser and long-term decisions which will be the true foundation for your business.

Additional optional sections:

- Expense by region, by market segment
- Revenue and sales projections by my company, by partners
- Sales by region, by segment

The End

I hope you found this book to be a helpful guide to create your marketing plan! I wish you success in everything you do and hope that the strategies in this book bring you closer to what you are trying to accomplish.

FURTHER FREE RESOURCES

Gift 1: I will give you one free online business/marketing course of YOUR choosing.

I teach 100+ online courses on business and marketing. I will give you one for absolutely free just for being a reader of this book, and you get to choose which one. Browse my full list of courses and email me telling me which course you want, and I will send you a coupon code to get into the course for free!

Here is my full list of courses:

https://www.udemy.com/user/alexgenadinik/

Send me an email to alex.genadinik@gmail.com and tell me that you got this book (so that I know why you are asking for a free course), and which of my courses you would like.

Gift: 2: Get my Android and iPhone business apps for free.

My apps come as a 4-app course and on Android and iPhone. I have free versions of each! All my free apps can be found on my website:

http://www.problemio.com

Here are a few links to the individual apps:

Free business plan app:

https://play.google.com/store/apps/details?id=com.problemio.two&hl=en

Free marketing app:

https://play.google.com/store/apps/details?id=com.marketing&hl=en

Free app on fundraising and making money:

https://play.google.com/store/apps/details?id=make.money&hl=en

Free business idea app:

https://play.google.com/store/apps/details?id=business.ideas&hl=en

Gift 3: Free business advice

If you have questions about your marketing or anything mentioned in this book, email me at alex.genadinik@gmail.com and I will be happy to help you. Just please keep two things in mind:

1) Remind me that you got this book and that you are not just a random person on the Internet.

2) Please make the questions clear and short. I love to help, but I am often overwhelmed with work, and always short on the time that I have available.

Thank you for reading and please keep in touch!

ABOUT THE AUTHOR

Alex Genadinik is a software engineer, self-made successful entrepreneur, prominent online business teacher, and a whiz marketer. Alex is a 3-time best selling Amazon author. His work has helped millions of entrepreneurs. You can learn more about Alex's current projects on his website: http://www.problemio.com

Alex has a B.S in Computer Science from San Jose State University.

Alex is also a prominent online teacher, and loves to help entrepreneurs achieve their dreams.

Here is a full list of books by Alex Genadinik on Amazon:
http://www.amazon.com/Alex-Genadinik/e/B00I114WEU

Here is a shortened URL for the full list of books:
https://goo.gl/uKk98y

Made in the USA
Las Vegas, NV
25 June 2023

73880567R10046